CW00742428

Throwback

SELECTED WORKS OF JAMES KIRKUP

The Submerged Village
A Correct Compassion
A Spring Journey
The Descent into the Cave
The Prodigal Son
Refusal to Conform
A Bewick Bestiary
Zen Gardens (photo-etchings with Birgit Skiöld)
Paper Windows: Poems from Japan
White Shadows, Black Shadows: Poems of Peace and War
The Body Servant: Poems of Exile
Scenes from Sesshu (photo-etchings with Birgit Skiöld)
To the Ancestral North: Poems for an Autobiography
Cold Mountain Poems
Scenes from Sutcliffe (portfolio of poems and photographs)
The Tao of Water (photo-etchings with Birgit Skiöld)
Miniature Masterpieces of Yasunari Kawabata
Insect Summer (children's novel)
The Magic Drum (children's novel)
The Love of Others
The Only Child: An Autobiography of Infancy
Sorrows, Passions & Alarms: An Autobiography of Childhood
These Horned Islands: A Journal of Japan
Tropic Temper: A Memoir of Malaya
Filipinescas
Streets of Asia
No More Hiroshimas: Poems & Translations
Selected Poems of Takagi Kyozo
Modern Japanese Poetry
Zen Contemplations
The Guitar Player of Zuiganji
Dengonban Messages: One-Line Poems
Ecce Homo - My Pasolini: Poems & Translations
Fellow Feelings
The Sense of the Visit: New Poems
Gaijin on the Ginza: A Novel
I, of All People: An Autobiography of Youth
A Poet could not but be Gay: Some Legends of my Lost Youth
Me All Over: Memoirs of a Misfit (Spring 1992)

James Kirkup

Throwback

Poems towards an Autobiography

Rockingham Press
1992

Published in 1992
by
The Rockingham Press
11 Musley Lane,
Ware, Herts
SG12 7EN

Copyright © James Kirkup 1992

British Library Cataloguing-in-Publication Data

A catalogue record for this book
is available from the British Library

ISBN 1 873468 03 2

Printed in Great Britain
by Bemrose-Shafron (Printers) Ltd., Chester

Printed on Recycled Paper

Supported by the Eastern Arts Board

To Akiko Takemoto -
with thanks for her many years
of friendship and support

Acknowledgments

Some of these poems have appeared in *Encounter*, *The Times Literary Supplement*, *The London Magazine*, *The New Yorker*, *Ambit*, *The Listener*, *The New Statesman*, *The Spectator*, *The Poetry Review*, *New Poetry*, *The Urban Gorilla*, *Orbis*, *Poetry Durham*, *Iron* and various anthologies.

Contents

Epigraph

Continent, city, country, society:
the choice is never wide and never free.
And here, or there ... No. Should we have stayed at home,
wherever that may be?

Elizabeth Bishop
Questions of Travel

Lost Soul

JK aged three, outside Granny Johnson's house in Robertson Street, South Shields

Lost Soul

(On a picture taken in childhood)

No camera could ever catch again
this visage, old before its time,
nor shutter the primeval rage
for solitude and silence in
the absent social stance.

No tyrant power could exploit
that vulnerableness, no chemical expose
its tender invisibility, nor print
the cat's wary nonchalance
in an affected poise.

Even when as here, in early childhood,
I defenceless stand, yet
obscurely armoured in my undivided gaze —
a child alone, framed in a doorway:
a front of detestation in a scowl of pain.

Eyes lowering but straight,
brow big, mouth still unschooled in smiles,
a little Taurus, about to butt his horns
against a wrong already half-expected,
in a life already far too long.

The left fist clenched, in desperation,
as if for a battle he
knew in advance not worth the fight.
(One blue eye, the right, is indeed
already bruised and blackened.)

Baffled as an aborigine
afraid to lose, with the taking
of his likeness, an emergent soul:
a veiled yet penetrating gaze
sunk in the sadness of primordial woe.

Wary of strangers' smiles,
suspicious of their ease, their looks,
of hands bearing gifts, caresses;
yet gulled with promises of beads,
baubles, toys broken as soon as touched.

Knowing himself a fool, and like a primitive
in love with all that was frivolous, shining.
Unable to distinguish dream from life,
false from true, good from bad —
perhaps not wishing to.

.

I knew it from the start,
and see now how much wiser I was then:
I am all there, the essence
of the boy I cannot mask.
— That child the father

of this man, that stocky dwarf
this delicate giant, that brave bull
this stricken deer, that dead David
this Jonathan — and this Goliath with
the stone embedded in his brow.

.

He sees it now: the pattern and
the picture of a life, a death —
something that did not have to be
but that a flash ordained as past and future
somewhere round the age of three.

Notes for an Autobiography

It was all decided long ago.
The split face, the mind divided,
the body growing in its own inevitable way,
the gloomy sex ambiguous in the dust
of time, the ever-shaken heart.

Was it to be for this that I was born?
My childhood was a corner of the back yard,
a crevice filled with sooty sand, a water-butt
black in the straight-edged sun that burned
the bricks and left the shadows by the window cold.

It was the chill of a dark and cobbled lane.
I walked blind to school through steaming glades
of sodden blankets, down the hill of trams,
through streets of coal and sand,
into an iron gate, an iron yard, a classroom like a clinic.

And all the while the mother and father watching,
caring, loving and refusing, scolding, giving.
There was more than melancholy in my wish for death.
It was a love of freedom, finally to be myself
even though it meant I should myself be lost.

Clutched the indifferent pennies in my narrow hand.
The shop was warm and dim, the biscuits, bread and vinegar,
the bins of flour, scoops, scales, butter-pats and cheese-wire,
tea, tins, jars and hanging hams, weights, measures, eggs
and custard, sweets, candied peel, potatoes, sugar.

— Desire's scorpion, hidden in the dusty privet
in the street's winter games, under the long lamplights
of the north, playing at plots and murders, enemies
in words and loving deeds.   The hands that clasped
the clinging knees, the silent gardens, bliss like summer rain.

Throwback

What mysterious genetic labyrinth has tracked my clue
to this off-centre? What secret ancestry
from pasts long distant, hidden in the memory?

Children often fantasize a changeling fate,
refusing to believe that they belong to
parents so different from themselves.

In my case, it was no fantasy, but a belief in
myself, my real place — inward conviction of apartness
that made me feel a stranger in our house.

Out of working class banality and poverty
why was it, when I caught a glimpse of
other ways of life, of modest luxury,

my eyes would fill with tears, regret, as if
I recognized, from some unchronicled era of the world,
the clear authority of my forgotten birthright?

In later years, my sense of strangeness among others
made me feel I was a visitor from outer space
to a society so utterly foreign, where I had no identity.

— What was my real source, the root of loneliness,
of what, despite all difficulties and discouragements,
I always knew I could not help becoming?

I know now I am that freak of fate, a throwback, reversion
cast so far from past into present that it has no name,
and neither family nor fortune could explain its mystery.

The Changeling

Here, in the long summer morning, played
the vanished gods.
Beneath the horrid cliff
the ruined sand is dark
still with their dancing.
Here they lay and wrestled, sang
and sprang with the hurdling breakers
in sunny glades that swept the spray
in slow-falling veils from the collapsing
pedestals of cliff, and from the waves'
hanging gardens, whose fountain-tops extinguished
fixed horizons with their leaping, spectral green.

    Here, hand in hand, we ran
    along the singing sands that like a smooth
    stone shone at the sea's retreating touch,
    making a double marvel of those golden games,
    whose alchemy reduced what should have been
    our shadow to a sharp reflection.

But all, now, are gone.
Like any criminal, in secret I have come
to find again that gay perfection that the world
rejects, to leap with them again
the crashing rainbows of the forbidden rocks.
But all, they are all gone.
The sun is low, and long shadows slide
like closing doors across the beaches,
locking in more than ice the wintry sea, whose arches
topple their dark and evening-reddened
crests of cloud like cornices of marble dust
with dry, hollow sounds along the crumpled shore.

    O, what an outcast I have now become
    since those deep summer days, when in my hand
    I held the clew and magic properties of love,
    and in a haunted morning slumbered my mortality away

upon immortal shoulders!   Where,
where are you now, companions of earth and air?

Will you return
again?   Return, you happy wonders,
and do not leave me like a stranger,
darkling!   Run from the neighbouring bay
with shouts of greeting and a wreath
of sea-flowers, air and foam ...   For since I knew
your wisdom, tenderness and grace,
I am a mortal lost among immortal memories,
caught in the war of dreaming and the world,
stranger to both.   O let the dove
of my deliverance within this drowning wave be bright,
and give my changed heart freedom from its stranger love.

Trow Rocks: January 1948

The Resurrected Man: Tollund

Inhabitant of my ancestral land,
he lay two thousand years in peat,
tanned by the earth's dark sun
and by the soil's cold heat.

The peasant cutter found him
buried in the sodden bog they mine
for fire, a braided rope around his neck:
a sacrifice to earth, a monument to time.

He wore the victim's foolish cap,
the cloak of nakedness. In earth's womb
he crouched like a full-grown foetus,
a ghost laid out in death's unfurnished tomb.

He stayed there as he fell in death:
his feet crossed, as if in sleep,
to bring him warmth and comfort;
his eyes closed, his breathing deep.

Then he was roused, uplifted by
the living man, unhoused by his own
descendants, who dissected his repose,
registered his fingerprints, and bared each bone.

Still he remained himself, preserved the archaic
dignity far older than his nails and eyes
and the heartsease and sorrel of his bed: an unimpregnable
acceptance — the faith that is the earth's where nothing dies.

Tollund, Denmark: 1950

Tyneside

Tyneside, 1936 by Humphrey Spender

The Town where I was Born

At the mouth of a great river rising to the sea
my town was both single and double, here and there,
the North and South, divided by the Tyne.

They were two separate entities, belonging
to different counties, having different speech,
yet united by a name's common denominator.

There was no bridge, no tunnel between the two.
Travelling from South to North Shields and back
we still have to pay our obolus and take the ferry

which to me was a first release, a breath of freedom,
delivering me from home and bringing my disquiet
"ower the watter" to a town familiar but strange.

It was always an enchanted voyage — in storm and calm,
rain and shine — to that other dream place. I was happy
to be leaving, less happy to be returning home.

Those almost daily voyages between my North and South,
loaded with lust and library books and scribbling pads —
presaging later partitions of desire between East and West.

·　·　·　·　·

And now I see it was from that divided town, that Scylla
and Charybdis my lightning-struck divisions came —
the ambiguities of being, thought and action.

It tugged my heart, my loyalties, my dreams, my passions
in opposite directions — made me both love and hate
the sundered town beside the sea, beneath colossal skies,

made me both cherish and abhor my roots, my origins,
my faults, my gifts, and even life itself. I became that ferry
on the great river rising to a sea of doubt and death.

Yet that separation from myself was very nature, an integrity
of twin poles united in a schizoid geography's connected
disconnections — the great river ever dividing, joining —

great river of memory rising to the vast, the open sea.

Tyneside, 1936

(a photograph of Humphrey Spender)

Darkness falling on the dead
quiet of the Quayside cobbles
where groups of laid-off men
in overcoats and flat black caps
are killing time, sad silhouettes,
lost shades waiting for the pubs to open.

The goods train tracks all lead
into the empty river, lit by a dying
winter sky's chaotic clouds, on which
the Victorian High Level and the static
black rainbow of the Great Tyne Bridge
define a total absence of animation.

Those men with useless hands in empty pockets
walk silently into the growing mists.
The Swing Bridge will not swing for them;
the distant lorries unloading beer barrels,
the moored freighter with smokeless stack
echo their aimlessness, a hopeless peace.

Among those groups of bitter ghosts, without
a job, without a name, waiting for another war,
is that my dead father I see walking there?

Tyne Ferry: Night

The turnstile's enigmatic tongue
reluctantly announces the impending passage.
Row-boats nibble at the long,
floating body of the landing-stage.

The passengers embark, anonymous
beneath the swinging arc-lamp's
gesticulating melodrama. Their elastic shadows
rage suddenly and vanish down the heaving ramps.

From the leaning smoke-stack, cables
of heroic steam are hauled. The broken
water glitters when departure's
hidden bells are shaken.

The boat gently valses, and a course is set
across the unseen harbour's springing darkness.
Louder the winds leap through the black proscenium of night,
and slowly now the landing's floodlit emptiness

glides like the setting for a nameless play
with sinister, deceptive urgency away.

View from the North-East

Across the end of every street the piled-up sea,
the sky and the indelible horizon stretch
like some faintly stirring backcloth, in front of which
the pillar-box, the street lamp and the tree detach
their elemental shapes with spectral poignancy.

Against a background of breakers that detonate
with soft explosions over the damp-stained beaches,
and throw up gulls in clouds of spray; the churches,
roof-tops, waterfronts and salt-cellar lighthouses,
ruins, a deserted bandstand, a broken fort

glide like cut-out toys over panoramic lakes.
A child moves like a ghost across the pink-cemented promenade,
and drags her solitary shadow like a lifeless weed
along the wave-ribbed edges of the sea, where hard
cirrus sand-shapes blanch at every step she takes.

Beach Road, South Shields, 1945

View from the Town Hall, South Shields

At the end of the narrow, empty room
the entire window, before the drawing of the blinds,
strains like a membrane to contain the sky,
or like a quartered sail upon a mast of air
swells with the coming night, the clouded winds.

Like a vast water-colour framed in bone,
the last blue rectangles of dusk begin
to overlap and darken.   The iron Hermes on the dome
dissolves, and unseen statues that with evening rain
will shine beneath the lamps, begin now to exchange

their daylight postures for the attitudes of night.
A balustrade continually crumbles out of sight
into the park's drowning trees, that cover and uncover
shaking stars, an avenue of lamps, a lighted ship's
descending constellation.   The clock-tower rises out of falling

waves of traffic, laughter, seas of brick, and streets
of rustling sand.   Like a strange face pressed inconveniently close
to mine, the changing features tell, with changeless tick
and tock, that now is forever now.   But at no other time
will it be quite the same — the winter loneliness, and four o'clock.

138, Fowler Street

The Sand Artist

JK at Whitstable in the summer of 1955

Landscape near Seaton Delaval

Coming from the sea, across the coal-streaked sands,
ascend the dunes, where sharp grass
shivers in monotonous north-easters.
Then you will see those heaps of slag that form
a mountainous province of perfect cones.

There, in the winter sea-mist,
while the foghorn moans
and perishes among the breakers,
the pit-head winding-gear hauls down,
on twinkling wheels, a sky of stone.

It was the larger landscape Vanbrugh saw —
the dunes, the sea, the fields of fog,
and he composed, for its romantic emptiness,
these rusticated towers, pillars, pediments,
ghosted the balustrades with statues, piled the steps.

Now, stranded among the rubbish of a drastic age,
its grandeur is more than ever strange, yet true.
Our only fantasies are violent.   Though a more decent
inequality prevails, we still require that state
of mind that can compose a monument to permanence.

When shall we learn again to trust the larger
landscape, life's underlying poise, discovering
another world, and other mountains, and another sun?
What is the right behaviour that can still secure
our flimsy world, and see eternity within its ruin?

Seaton Sluice

The Sand Artist

On the damp seashore
above the rainbows of shells, seaweed, seacoal,
the sandman wanders, seeking for a pitch.

Ebb-tide is his time. The sands are lonely,
but a few lost families
camp for the day on its Easter emptiness.

He seeks the firm sand of the retreating wave.
They, with their sandwiches and flasks of tea,
lay their towels upon the dry slopes of dunes.

From the sea's edge he draws a pail
of bitter brine, and carries it carefully
towards the place of first creation.

There he begins his labours. Silent,
not looking up at passing shadows
of curious children, he moulds his dreams.

No simple sandcastles, melting as they dry,
but galleons, anchors, liners, cornucopias,
mermaids, Neptunes, dragons of the deep.

With a piece of stick, a playing card
and the blunt fingers of a working man
the artist draws existence into being from the sea.

As the returning tide takes back his gifts,
he waits in silence by his pitman's cap
for pennies from the sky.

Ocean Road sands

South Shields: Winter

Here at the calm sea's edge
the slow, wide waves
lasso the melancholy beach
with long, curving ropes
of gleaming sand, bring into reach
dry festoons of weed,
flotsam left by a summer tide.

If you could only throw, sea,
your circles wide enough,
you could so quietly engulf
the privet in the parks, the pink-paved
promenade, the flash arcade
and the entire town behind.
— No one would know.   No one would really mind.

Trow Rocks

Mornings in Whitby

Smoke from smouldering sea-coal,
bitter, harsh and salty as the air
veils the grey slate roofs,
the harbour lamps, the quays, the steps,
the figures on the dreaming bridge.

The waters of the early morning tide
wash the harbour with the tranquil light
that lies also on misted tiles
from which whole families
of chimneys rise, working ghosts of brick.

The Watering Carts of Summer

In the dogdays, so few,
so rare in our northern summer by the sea,
a small tram, its only passenger a water tank
toured all the sand-swept town, sprinkling
the overheated, dusty tracks
with slow, gentle downpours.

Another, a tank on a cart pulled by a horse,
ambled round the cobbled side-streets
followed by crowds of barefoot kids
and a pack of lost, panting dogs.
— But what I remember best of all
is the sweet scent of the air after it passed.

Durham seen from the Train

The cathedral glides behind the cutting's
long wave of grass and earth, removed
completely by a window's fractional displacement
and the locomotive's endless moment
that closes like a wall now on the flower-foamed
embankment, now on a bird's unmoving wings.

The traditional escarpment
crumbles out of sight.   The prison
and the hollow castle fall upon their knees.
The river turns and disappears into a crust of trees.
The last houses like a rib lie broken
on a temporary field invaded by a token pavement.

The heart imagines what the eye no longer sees.
Though distance seems to kill the things we love
and time preserves the gift beyond the giver,
still in a moment's bead of air the lover
lives within his kiss, hand treasures hand forever; and above
the reappearing river still the city rises where it always rose.

The Elementary School Class Photo

Class IV of Westoe Elementary School

Self-Portrait with Teddy Bear

In my dark high-necked cable-knit sweater,
the one my mother knitted and I soon grew out of,
I am sitting up straight in a photographer's
unreal studio, posed against a painted background
of formal garden with a bit of classic stone balustrade.

My fair hair, of modest length, is parted on the left
on a wide, calm brow: the eyes are clear, dark blue,
intense, the nose a joke still, ears enormous,
the mouth small, compressed, determined.
I'm obviously conscious of the importance of the pose.

I'm trying hard to hold it, to sit straight, keep still.
— That's no problem for the big stout teddy bear
whom I hold loosely with both hands on my right knee
(he's just a prop, the photographer's, not mine).
He leans confidingly his round plush head

against my right shoulder, ears prominent like my own,
candidly displaying the soles of his flat, clumsy feet
and the neat brown pads of his stumpy paws, his stitched
mouth, bright eyes fixing the camera intently
with the same cool expectant look as mine. But not so blue.

The Elementary School Class Photo

Against a wall of grimy brick with a rotten drainpipe
our class of twenty-four nine-year-olds, all boys,
is kneeling, sitting or standing — the top six
tall on a bench along the back of the group.
They are the ones from the betterclass families,
lads good at football, cricket, sums, exams.

We are framed on either side by the portly, white-haired
headmaster with his draped watch-chain (he's the kindly one
who used to cane me unmercifully — six on each palm —
for refusing to salute the Union Jack on Empire Day),
and by our teacher, Twentyish, but no shingled flapper,
in strapped shoes, low-buttoned coat, fur-trimmed sleeves.

My classmates nearly all have criminal faces, or look
mentally retarded, dressed in jerseys, worn jackets,
hair fixed with tapwater, striped school ties askew.
I can still remember their faces, their names —
Harvey, Marks, Ritsema, Foreman, Bobby Diamond —
all real lads, good for a fight at the gates after school.

There is one here, too, with his simple moon-face,
whom they all tormented, and who patiently died
of mute despair among those animal thugs and crooks —
wide boys lost in war, dropped dead at factory or office.
I remember all their tricks, their voices, their smells.
I can even remember exactly where some of them lived —

the nobs in detached houses, with gardens on new estates,
the rest of us in slums, vanished rows of coal-smoked brick
near the gas-works, the pit, the cemetery, the biscuit factory.
— Fifty years on, I wonder now if any of them can remember one
kneeling in the front row, among the dunces, the dole kids,
with a girl's pale face and hair, and a black eye?

Snowballs

I saw Russian children throwing snowballs
at Yehudi Menuhin — all in good clear fun,
of course, though the snows of Leningrad
were far from clean that sunless winter day.

The master, whom as a child I had envied so,
took it all in good part, not even
bothering to brush the icy stars away
from his fur hat — though in the end
he was standing half-hidden by a tree trunk,
and the smile on his lips had become
frozen, hunted.   Fear shone in his gentle eyes.

My heart went out to him, and to the memory
of childhood terrors at the sight of snow
on winter mornings when I had to go to school.
The fantasies of freshly-fallen snow,
the weaving and drifting of those airy flakes —
the transformation of our dull, dark northern town
into another world, a lost paradise I recognized
as mine: that was a magic I could gaze upon
for hours on end from our front room window bay.

But it was a treacherous delight, a trap
for the solitary child, he who never joined
in games or gangs, the lost outsider,
the queer outcast quieter and paler than the snow,
who trod with fearful footsteps on the way to school
the most obscure back lanes, the least expected route
taken by no others, an imaginative map
beyond the pale — a geography only he explored.

He lingered, hiding behind dustbins, telegraph poles,
or darting into strange back yards, dark coal houses
and fragrant netties, to escape the hunters
heard shouting just around a corner — his heart
thudding loudly in that self-made silence
till they had passed, those tough boys and tougher girls
to whom he never would belong, who did not want him.

Then, when the coast seemed clear, the danger less,
crept to the iron gates of school: in time for the bell,
the classes lined up neatly in the shattered snows
between brick walls scarred with splintered ice of battles.

     *   *   *

But on the homeward road they lay in wait for him
outside the cruel gates — and no master to defend him.
The snowballs flew like stones, like winter birds
smashing with folded wings against a wall of glass,
pelting his apartness, his difference, his frailty
with violences worse than any words, or any names —
banging his ears, his eyes, his mouth gasping in shock
as the stone-centred bullets struck his back, his heart.
— And no dreamed-of best friend to come and rescue him ...

"Fight back! Fight back!" The parents urged him out
into the lamplit street, and stood together there
behind the bay window's curtains of dusty lace,
watching the street boys launch their icy avalanches.

He stood outside the open front door, looking for help
towards that curtained window from which no help came:
then ran back inside, into the warmth and safety
of a home that felt no longer warm and safe.
For they, too, father and mother both, seemed enemies
and looked at their coward son in scorn and silence
as he shook, in the gaslit kitchen, his wounds of war
from the snow-battered coat and cap, and tried to smile.
— Then fled to the dark chill of the front room window bay,
to weep in secret as he watched those others out at play.

     *   *   *

I never forgot that evening, that betrayal
as the street lamps turned my tears to stars of gold
among the falling flakes of airy snow. And from that night
I kept my life, my thoughts, my dreams, apart from them,
so that they had to find a word that would explain
my alteration, my silences, my secret life: "diffident."
What they really meant, I know, was "different."

Years later, in Leningrad, I watched the snowballs
batter Yehudi Menuhin — all in good clean fun, of course —
Of course. And felt my heart go out to one who, great and famous,
became the hounded child I was in winter, in the cruel north,
the Tyneside ghetto of my loneliness, my endless fears.

Brownie Box Camera

That acrid smell, vaguely
pharmaceutical, chemmy lab stink
of its matt-black interior
still haunts my nostrils
with childish fanatasies of
opium, chloroform, paregoric.

The artificial black lizard skin
of the oblong box, in which
I clipped that first clumsy roll
of crimson film, cranking it till No.1
surfaced through the round, red
celluloid eye — unwinking stare.

The muted colours in
the misty viewfinder had
a soft impressionist charm.
I trained it on shipyard, slag heap,
mine, lighthouse, our back lane,
bandstand, ruined windmill, cliffs.

The milkman with his swinging churn,
the coalman with his scales,
neighbours, teachers, friends,
all were subjects for my vision of
our town. — But those dreamy pastels
came out black, white and grey.

Dreaming of Dead Parents

JK with his mother and father in the garden of their later home at Flemish Buildings, Corsham, near Bath.   A photograph taken by J.R. Ackerley

A Letter from my Mother

The address on the envelope
is in a strange hand.
You had to ask a stranger
to write the Japanese address for you —
but I know it comes from you.

Inside, the sheet of paper
is carefully folded. Your hands
are still tender to the things they touch,
and even gentler than when I was a child.
Your hand smoothed it as you did my brow, my hair.

You tell me the small daily happenings
of your ordered life — the visits
to and from friends, the unexpected
distant relative's call, a car drive in the hills,
your lonely wanderings in the streets of Bath.

How you smelled the flowers in the gardens,
crushed leaves of geranium, mint, verbena
between those delicate worn fingers:
ladslove, mignonette, lavender and thyme,
rosemary, catnip — they are your inseparables.

How you love the night-scenting stock by the river,
the rustle of willows along the dark canal,
the chirp of sparrows and the song of starlings
on your windowsill, the grumbling of doves
and lorries among the chestnuts bordering the park.

Braving the traffic, you step off the pavement
like a queen confident that all gives way before you
— and all gives way. Kind hands and arms
hold you, guide you like my constant thoughts
across the roads no others dare to cross.

Sometimes you try to write yourself
a letter whose thoughts you could dictate to no one
and tell only to me. You use a black metal board
with its horizontal black elastic guidelines
and write as best you can, unseeing, with your heart.

I can always read your meaning, even when,
interrupted, you did not know where you left off.

Nagoya, 1971

38

Dreaming of Dead Parents

From time to time, they come to me,
mother and father, in a long and vivid dream.
I go to meet them in a town
both familiar and strange — a curious mixture
of all the towns we knew,
yet better known to them than me.

They come to meet me, young and smiling,
a handsome couple, to bring me laughter, talk,
and a sense of consolation in distress, or loss,
or loneliness. Or we meet when they are old,
and blind: and, as I used to do,
I guide my mother's steps around the streets of Bath,
a town grown strange to her, and new to me.
I take my father's hand, and he
smiles back at me with love and admiration, as once he did.
We walk along the heights above the Tyne,
or down the mile-long pier, where my mother stands,
laughing, great clouds of spray exploding right over her.

Wherever we are, on both their faces I can recognize
an unforced sweetness, the candour of their gaze
when we were happy once together,
careless in my childhood days.

Such dreams are the rewards of sleep and death.
I see in them our true selves, more wise and patient
than when we were awake, and living.
— Those dreams to me are proof of an eternity,
of death's own kind of life, a perfect anarchy
where we have gone beyond the blindness and
the weakness of the day, into
a night of radiance, peace, communion,
in which the dead know all, and forgive all, completely:
and understand us, lonely sufferers left behind,
with a pure morality, beyond all dogma, beyond all law.

In Memory of my Mother Mary

You have just run round to
the corner shop — gone
on an errand only you can manage,
a message I could never run for you.

Gone for half a loaf, a twist of tea,
a pat of butter and an ounce of cheese;
gone with pride and a smile
to bring me a banquet.

No one ever knew
when you were hard-up.
Your pride and gentleness
were classic in their simplicity.

You worked for me
as I could never work for you —
I carried out the ashcan to the lane,
but it was you who lit the fire.

I cleaned the grate and shovelled coal,
but it was you who bore
the burden of my loneliness,
and gave the purity no sin could blacken.

'And I've never been out of the country,'
you used to say, but unresentfully, listening
in later years to tales of travel.   Well,
my dear, you're out of it now, thank God,

gone on a journey I have still to make
and that my father made before us.
He knew the way, and showed you
how to go, as I know he will show me.

The last time I saw you
was in your best suit and hat,
after our day out, standing
smiling goodbye between two nurses.

The poet's mother as a young woman.

You stood between them
waving to the son you could not see,
as the lift moved upwards as if to heaven:
a last ascension, that leaves me lost

in loneliness far deeper, darker than
ever as a child or as a youth I knew.
— There is no loneliness where you have gone,
but only thankfulness, and duty done.

On a Photograph of my Father
as a Young Man

The canvas backcloth is a bare
conservatory with one heavy palm,
      the kind of air
he never breathed; whose warm
and fragrant luxury was far
      from life or dream.

He faintly smiles beneath the new
moustache. His brow is fair,
      the look is true.
— What had he seen to mar
that calm with sadness, mark the blue
      eyes with despair?

Was it a warning of the truth,
of the necessity for courage
      as we find youth,
so strong, so hot with ease and rage,
hating the bitter taste within its mouth
      of grief and age?

The poet's father as a young man.

My Father's Rule

Brass-bound boxwood
with the two triple brass hinges
and, on the eighteenth inch,
the big brass sun,
the folding centre.

'Rabone Warranted Boxwood
Made in England
No. 1380.'

At the tenth and fourteenth inches
brass points fit into holes
at the twenty-second and twenty-sixth inches.
On the inner seventeenth and nineteenth inches,
two tiny brass pins protrude,
linking with holes on the thirty-fifth inch and the first,
the holes worn with use
into slits that cannot hold.

The four nine-inch lengths
smooth and neat
folding together, opening
like a fan: the noble numbers and
the halves, quarters, tenths —
dark on the outside,
dark with the labour and sweat
of my father's hands,
the inside numbers clearer,
the wood paler, like his palms.

•

When I was a boy
often I played for hours
with this rule —
opening it and shutting it,
folding it, extending it.

The rule became so many things to me —
the holding centre was a crown of gold,
a coin of undiscovered realms:
the steel rivet at its heart
was the hub of every thought and act.

Sometimes, a solitary child,

I unfolded it to make
the oriental zigzag fence
of our Willow Pattern plates.
Sometimes, opened upright
and covered with a duster
borrowed from my mother Mary
it became an American native wigwam.
Or it grew into a tree
of angled branches like an ancient plum —
in my imagination
I could make anything
of its flexible inflexibility.
                    •

Three feet of honesty and pride
in decent workmanship —
thirty-six inches divided into four
stained, worn wooden slats
that measured more than wood.

The hands of the carpenter have blessed them,
and the skill of the craftsman hallowed them
all the days of his life.
For every time he used them
he gave them grace, his touch
each day was left upon them,
part of his very self —
in work and out of it.

I see still the way he used to slide his folded rule
into the long side pocket of his dungarees,
and how, as he strode along,
it knocked against his thigh.

I see him draw it out to measure
my height, marked on the door-jamb each birthday
by his flat carpenter's pencil with its chisel point.

Now, a lost child,
and more alone than ever,
I hold my father's rule
in helpless hands, holding it for dear life,
and holding on to it, like grim death,
a last plank in
the wreck of a drowning world.

— And where is his spirit level now?   *July 23, 1977*

45

My Father's Toolbox

He made it for himself,
the first proof
of grave apprenticeship,
the lad good with his hands
and awkward with his feet.

He made it to last
all his days, as solid as a ship,
the ship he longed to sail away on
but that never came to port.
It still endures, beyond his days.

It lies now on the shelf
in our garden shed, collecting dust.
It seems to mock the son
who could never use it — solid
as a roof, or a coffin.

My Grandmother's Tea-Set

On the rustic pink and white checked tablecloth
fine white china, the prim teacup handles
just flecked with gilt on top, just so;
the rims of plates and cups and saucers
all looped with a thin gilt line, hand-painted.

In the centre of each plate, the sugar-bowl side,
and on each cup's slightly-curving lip, just where
I put my mouth to drink, a gilt shamrock,
simple trefoil that always brought me luck, like the silver
threepenny-bit in my slice of Sunday seed cake.

*With Granny Kirkup in her garden at West Avenue,
Harton, South Shields in 1930.*

My Grandmother's Weatherglass

Barometer was too grand a word
for her, Anna Maria, the simple soul,
who found it was perhaps too difficult
to pronounce in her soft East Anglian burr.

It used to hang at the foot of the stairs
in her house at the top of Ada Street,
next to the scented porch's stained glass door,
and every morning she would tap the glass

to see what the weather was going to be — just
as she did when she was young, and married to
her Viking clipper captain, making the China run
for tea, silk, porcelain — to Shanghai, Yokohama,

Hong Kong, Singapore, Canton, Formosa.
— How she dreaded news of tempests, and
our north-eastern gales that she was sure
must blow, too, across the China Seas!

It is the one memory of her that I possess:
its round, moon-like face, like hers,
innocent and kind, and primly Victorian —
this old cracked glass she would tap, then sigh ...

The dial runs the whole gamut of my life:
Stormy, Rain, Change, Fair, Very Dry,
with temperatures ranging from Fahrenheit
to Centigrade, as my father explained to me.

Such a battered, dented, black old metal case!
She told me it had made the run to eastern ports
in my grandfather's *Nina*, wrecked off Tsushima,
or in his schooner named the *Wanderer*.

It, too, was a wanderer like himself
on his first ship, a brig carrying coals
from Tyneside to Bordeaux, returning
cargoed with barrels and bottles of wine.

Then he gave her the Barometer, to comfort
her fears for him she loved when he was far away
in unimaginable seas, in deadly calms,
or in typhoons, ungovernable tropic storms.

It has wandered with me, too, companion
faithful as memory, from Tyne to Liffey,
from London to Malaya and Japan, where
it now hangs above my paper window.

— I inherited her husband's wandering spirit
that she would not let my father follow.
So I am really my grandfather's only son,
the one wanderer he would have wanted.

He died before my birth.   Drowned at sea.
One of his barometer's hands has fallen off,
but the other is stuck at Change — (for Changeable,
my grandmother told me) — the only weather in my life.

My Mother's Knitting

I often feel that memory, the comfort
of her freshly-knitted socks
on my boy's feet — how soft, luxurious,
so firm, warm, yet cool — how they seemed made
to hold my steps with gentlest love.

My mother knitting by the fire, hour after hour,
as I sat reading: her four steel needles winking
in the flickering flames, the magic gaslight;
their quiet clicking, every stitch and turn
became in her fingers a work of art, slow and patient.

And gloves too. The ones she secretly knitted
from old, unravelled wool for my Christmas present
that long winter of my thirteenth year —
first putting them on, that snowy Christmas morning,
was like putting on her own hands, so close, so tender.

Socks, gloves, mufflers, Fair Isle sweaters, cast on,
cast off, all these she made for me alone, so soon
worn out, lost, tossed carelessly away.
— Now all I have of them, and her, one precious relic,
is this persistent memory of their comforting.

Patterns

Where has everything I remember vanished?
Where is it now, that comforting quilt, the one
my mother stitched for her trousseau,
in wartime, and under which I was conceived,
well over seventy years ago?

It was the colour of fresh cream,
the cotton cover always cool and soft.
My mother's tiny stitches — months of work —
divided it patiently into leaf and lozenge,
thousands of pinpoint holes, so neat, so perfect.

It was always laid on top of their double bed.
Sometimes, after a night of asthma, in early childhood
I would lie on top of it, and sleep so securely:
then wake in time for tea by the kitchen fire,
my pale face stamped by her handiwork.

And at night, looking up at the sky with her
or with my father, above our sooty back yard,
I would trace her patterns in those pinpoint stars.
— Where has it all gone? Why do I suddenly need it,
that old quilt she made with love?

My Mother's Sewing

'Stitch! stitch! stitch!
In poverty, hunger, and dirt ...
Oh! God! that bread should be so dear,
And flesh and blood so cheap!'

Not for nothing you knew by heart
Thomas Hood's 'The Song of the Shirt' —

As you sewed my clothes beneath the gas
the incandescent gas mantle, or in the pale
daylight from the kitchen window
(the lace curtains drawn aside)
I listened to the rhythm, the steady beat
of the treadle of the treadle sewing machine,
the Singer sewing machine, the treadle on which
your neat foot untiringly danced its labours
as you smiled at me absorbed in my book,
or at my father home from work, reading
'The Gazette', or writing in his diary,
your eye upon my new shirt's unwavering seam
or stitching the buttonholes, as you recited:

'With fingers weary and worn,
With eyelids heavy and red,
A woman sat in unwomanly rags,
Plying her needle and thread —
Stitch! stitch! stitch! ...'

But Hood's words were just a joke to you,
and to my father and myself. Not for you
his Victorian sentimentality and melodrama,
but rather his serious wit, political (as you were)
without knowing it, unthinking socialist.

'Stitch! stitch! stitch!
In poverty, hunger, and dirt ...
Oh! God! that bread should be so dear,
And flesh and blood so cheap!'

And still in my attentive memory I hear
the heavy tread of the ornate metal treadle,
spring, summer, autumn, winter, and smell
the fresh scent of the unwashed cotton
as for the first time, entranced,
I pulled the new shirt over my head
and buttoned up the little pearl buttons,
buttons of mother-of-pearl — words that always
fascinated me, and fitted you, my mother —
my precious mother of pearl!

'Stitch! stitch! stitch!
Stitch! stitch! stitch! ...'

Ghosts in New Mexico

In the art museum at Santa Fe
I saw a ghost from my childhood —
black japanned, with gilt floral decorations,
my mother's Singer Sewing Machine
in all its elegant, cast-iron efficiency.

While you with gentle energy
trampled the fretted treadle — the metal
worn shiny by your neatly-shod foot —
and turned the fat little hand-wheel
with untiring hand, work-worn,

I sat beside you, at that shiny walnut drop-leaf
above the two oblong drawers with
their small inset wooden knobs,
my first writer's table, where later
I pencilled poem on poem for you.

How often I caught my prying fingers
in those sliding boxes filled with buttons
and bobbins, reels of Cash's Sylko-silken thread!
Or, sitting on the floor beside you, tried
to help your labour, pushing the treadle with my hands.

Your sweet smile full of pins,
you hummed snatches from "The Gondoliers,"
"Floradora", "The Belle of New York", "San Toy",
or from my grandfather's Irish drawing-room repertoire —
"Maritana", "The Bohemian Girl"

or arias from Verdi, Wagner, Offenbach —
that "Barcarolle" I hear so often now,
over-amplified, ignored by supermarket crowds,
but whose wave-rocked Venitian valse
gave then the very rhythm of our work.

— Japanned with light reflected from our curtained
kitchen window, the Singer was the idol of my days,
and of my nights, when I would sometimes dream of
its stabbing needle transfixing my index finger
on the busy shuttle, in a cloud of tangled thread.

Now, far from home, I see you seated there once more
on one of our old plush-seated parlour chairs,
your fair head bent above the well-stitched seam.
And, falling from your knees, a cataract of cotton for
my first pyjamas, or drifts of flannel for our winter shirts.

Dressing the Tree

We never had a real Christmas tree —
only a plastic one, but pretty, from Woolworth's,
with scarlet berries tipping the stiff boughs
of bright green needles.

We kept it on top of the tallboy, from one
year's end to the other, in its special box.
It folded up like a furry umbrella frame:
"Well, that's another year gone," my Dad would say.

But during Christmas week — not a day before —
we hauled it down and dusted it in the back yard.
Those artificial needles were glued on well:
they never fell — an authentic fir tree.

We stood it on the kitchen draining board
and straightened out the creaky boughs, one by one;
its rigid trunk was clamped into a white enamel pot,
the hard plaster sprayed with fake moss.

From another battered box we lifted out of tissue paper
our Christmas decorations — a sprinkler of glitterfrost,
the great glass globes of violet and orange, blue and crimson,
and carefully hooked them, like delicate fruit

among the ropes of gold and silver tinsel
upon those boughs that seemed to come alive
when at each tip we fixed a tiny candle
of white or pastel pink, each on a tin flower.

Next, we tied with rainbow ribbons round the pot
a fresh red crepe paper frill with cut-out snowflakes.
Then, at last, on the topmost twig, we ceremoniously
fastened a crumpled star of sparkling, sequinned satin.

Already our Christmas tree appeared to sing and dance
with more than plastic joy. — And only then, slowly, one
by one, we lit the candles, that illuminated our living tree
and our pale winter faces with warmth and gladness.

We always placed it on the little table
in our front room's bow window, the curtains open
so that all might see our shining star and feel its light
upon their lives, and share in our rejoicing.

Demolition and Nativity

Cockburn Street, South Shields during demolition in 1972. JK is looking from the window of the house where he was born, together with a cameraman from a television crew recording the event.

Visiting a Birthplace

In the street where I was born
the backlane walls are battlefields of bricks —
roofs ripped off slates and floorboards rived

windowpanes blasted by boys
doors hammered-in the knockers fled
flags upended cobbles scattered

drainpipes askew crashed chimneypots
split skulls on backyard steps the stacks
of blackened brick bashed in

the coalhouse mined the wash-house fire
damped with slag the copper plugged
with ash, broken jamjars, papers, rags.

•

The kitchen snecks are snapped,
the tub of sooty rain is busted.
The bolted netty gapes.

Our frontroom window still stands.
The sash is jammed, the fastener loose.
A ragged curtain of dusty lace blows through

black stars of shivered glass, my mother's woe.
— Its view of me has changed, but not
of the iron grate, the papered wall on which

as it always did, our northern sun
still casts above the mantlepiece
the shadow of a frame the joiner made.

Cockburn Street, South Shields, 1973

Demolition and Nativity

There is no other place
like the room we are born in.
The moment no one remembers
is enshrined in it for ever.

To see those walls and windows
smashed not by time and the elements,
but by workmen, boys, bombs, machines,
is to be torn alive.

— Yet not until I saw
the ruined shell that was my womb,
stripped and naked to the sky,
did I feel glad that I had lived.

Cockburn Street, South Shields

The Memory Palace

Wide wings curve from the main façade
that is the storehouse of childhood's
many staircases, growing narrower as they rise —
to the attics, or down to the basement
of desire's delays and disappointments.

In each dust-clothed, shuttered room
cupboards and closets packed with first impressions,
nearly always bad, and so unforgettable, though
a few good ones lie tucked away in empty tins
and chocolate boxes, high on back shelves.

The bedrooms are breaking voices, now soft,
now suddenly loud, of all the personal associations —
friends, lovers, parents, teachers, strangers, enemies —
and all the arcades are pillared with recesses
for a million words, alcoves of glittering images.

Radiating from the upper galleries are secret dens,
chambers bricked-off and full of horrors —
that working-class hang-up, nightmare shame,
fear of heights, dislike of soup, sermons; hatred
of other children, adoration of one's only self.

The kitchens are a circulating library of smells
and tastes, the bathrooms steamy with first sex,
the wardrobes full of furs, satins scented with mothballs
of morbid lust, the mahogany dresser drawers of dreams
packed with incriminating letters, drawings, drugs.

— But out in the landscaped acres of Italian gardens
at the end of the day's long avenue of cypresses,
behind a glass-fanged wall, the outhouses pungent with
the pine shavings of strange, forbidden, hidden loves:
the toolsheds of passion, perversity and poetry.

Meeting and Parting

JK in the garden of his house at Nagoya, Japan.

Dreams of Dead Lovers

They all keep coming back,
those gay insouciants, imposters
who once took up with me — a clown
forever fooled by his own foolish ecstasy —
although for them it was only, had I known,
a bit of a lark, good for a giggle.

And I was nothing much to them —
a warm body, a chat, a drink,
a cheap way of passing the time
when hard-up and nothing better offered,
soon dropped, a dead loss, a poor joke —
in folly ripe, in reason rotten.

Because they were always
so much younger, better looking,
better dressed, so good at games,
I appeared beside them, not it's plain,
as a seedy uncle but rather a maiden aunt
following with blind adoration, lonely pride

their every movement, every gesture
filled, it seemed, with inimitable grace.
— Now they come back to me in dreams,
often two of them together, in all their caddishness.
But I am still alive, remembering their charm, while they,
now dead, are doing what they always did so well — forgetting.

Meeting and Parting

In the deserted stone temple garden
I came to a small bridge,
and just as I was crossing the stream
a monk appeared from nowhere
and began to cross in the opposite direction.

The bridge was narrow —
but we passed one another comfortably
at the centre, giving a slight
bow, with lowered lids;
it was over in a second.

I walked on, off the bridge,
as he did, into the empty garden
that was far from empty for two
who had almost passed through one another
like wandering ghosts.

— From the moment of our birth
we had been walking towards
that moment of passage
on a bridge I had never crossed before —
an ordinary encounter.

So are all encounters, passages
through all our moments, though we do not know it,
from birth to death, on one long bridge,
in the empty stone gardens
of our crowded worlds.

Kyoto

Looking at Old Snapshots

in memoriam, R.L.

In a rusty Harrogate Toffee tin
I found this handful of curling negatives —
my childhood and youth in smoky reverse.

Holding them up to the light,
I could make nothing of their faded ghosts.
Whose could that head be, slightly
out of focus? What doorway was that? Our home?
The group upon the beach at Marsden,
the two schoolboys on bikes —
who were they all? And where
was I? ...
         Suddenly, I felt my heart
beating with childish excitement, my eyes
filled with tears of longing. — Would he
be among these ghosts, my lost love,
my drowned sailor, long since dead?

     •   •   •

Yes, at the camera shop, they told me —
Japanese experts at developing and printing —
it would be possible to print them, but
many were in bad condition — some
over fifty years old, others out of focus.
Would I want them all printed,
however poor the quality? Oh, yes,
yes, I begged them — print all.

     •   •   •

With shaking fingers, I opened
the wallet of shiny prints — mother,
hanging out washing in the back lane, father
digging the allotment, the Town Hall's
Paris Opera nudes surrounding Queen Victoria,
Frenchman's Bay, Trow Rocks,

the lighthouse, the corner shop,
our little front garden (the fence my father made
still stands there) — the crowds of the dead
in King Street, Ocean Road, the forgotten, the unknown.

But no — he
was not among them, my first love, the one
I had loved at fifteen with all my heart, loved
more than life itself, to his great amusement,
loved as I have never loved again —
and who had died without my knowing,
but still mocking my foolishness.

Venice Preserved

I glance in passing into
the freckled depths of this Venetian glass
aureoled in rusted crystal studs.
Against a sunny backdrop of the Grand Canal
I see a stranger's darkened face — darkened
by Italian suns, by the palazzo's awnings,
and by my sudden memories of long-lost love.

For this is where we stayed that year
while summer rotted into rainy autumn.
This was the very room, and this the glass
in which our faces smiled at one another
in nights of love, and days of tenderness.
In the mirror's room, we were together, imprisoned
in every moment, without care for winter in the wind.

Now as I pause, and gaze into the mirror's past,
I seem to see, beside my own reflection,
the face of one I loved, a ghost of passion.
— But also, swimming in the tainted depths,
so many other shapes, of visitants long dead,
the centuries of faces that reflected here,
and were reflected, as I am — we are — now.

They crowd upon the mirror's unretentive wave
and seem to dim its time-corrupted screen
as if their millions of smiles, glances, tears
had worn the silvery backing bare. — As they have worn
the visage of the Serenissima, the squat Basilica,
the very stones of Venice — Canaletto roofs and
Guardi squares, towers and arcades. The Bridge of Sighs.

The New Address Book

Why do I hang on to all this junk?
Half a dozen old address books
commemorating thirty years of people, places,
countries, continents and islands —
what use to me now?

Some of the names belong
to men and women completely forgotten,
with addresses I cannot imagine writing,
and mysterious telephone numbers
for calls never made.

Some belong to those who have gone away,
left home without a forwarding address.
Others, once deeply loved,
but somehow just dropped out of my existence
without a word of explanation.

Who were those long-ago acquaintances,
the friends and enemies, the haters and the lovers?
Where are they now? Do they sometimes think
of me, as I of them? I know that some
have gone forever into death, leaving no message.

My mother's last address — the room in Bath
she knew she would die in — I cannot bear
to cross it out, though it is seared on my memory,
as I cannot bear to let the others go, any of them.
— So I start copying them all out again, in

my mind and memory, hopefully,
and in my new address book.

Moves

The place stripped bare
looks as it did when first
I entered it, a homeless creature,
in the last months of that uncertain year
when the world's anger seemed about to burst,
and it became a useless gesture
to seek a roof, a window anywhere.

The months have passed,
and once again, a restless visitant,
I now prepare to bid my last
farewell to what will be my past —
that I have lived through, revenant
of solitude, without the least
sign of wisdom in the waste.

O, can you be the same
bare and uninhabitable place
as when I entered you, my room
that was a stranger, now become
a stranger once again, a face
empty of any welcome?
Is there no memory remains, no trace of time?

Or are you merely a sad
apartment of the outer light,
a grave of brick, a dusty bed
where no ghost will ever lay his head
and no future will be right —
its only visitants the mad
haunters of nothing, the living dead?

Newcastle upon Tyne

Poet as Sisyphus

JK at the age of 18.

Non-Fiction

'Poetry is the supreme fiction, madame ...'
                    Wallace Stevens

Biographies are not made up.
Even the most humdrum individuals
have humdrum lives that read
better than any novel, because
they are not made up.

Yet for that very reason
I dread the dreadful
bleak truth of the ending:
bitterness, loneliness, helplessness —
the decline and death of all
that was fresh, brilliant, careless,
defiant, courageous, lovable —
into such sickness, blindness, sadness,
into delusion, drunkenness, drugs, neglect,
into obscurity, poverty, suicide, murder.

In a novel, we accept these things,
because they are just made up.
But in real life, the life of
fellow human beings —
O Baudelaire, Cavafy, Pasolini, Proust,
Kafka, Keats, Kleist, Clare, Rimbaud —
reality more frightening than
the wildest nightmares, the most gothic ghosts —
O Marlowe, Mandelstam, Housman, Heine,
Leopardi, Chatterton, Firbank, Poe and Wilde —

No, I cannot read to the end of such lives,
nor face, as they either did or didn't,
the mounting decline.
Perhaps in such cases
it is better to read the ending first,
like some cheap detective story, though
not made up, without fiction —

the innocent revealed,
the murderer known from the start,
the victim identified.

Then, disabused, to begin again bravely,
fully aware of the fatal consequences
of ever having the bad luck to be born.

Poet as Sisyphus

Face glassy with sweat,
this human dung-beetle
rolls his useless burden
up a slope not far from horizontal.

Yet it takes every ounce of craft
to trundle it right to the top,
where, pausing to wipe his brow,
he sees it start to move
to move back down the slope,
so slowly, but with a force
as inert as its own weight —
inexorable gravity.

He lets it go. He knows too well
it's no use trying to restrain it,
to halt its earthbound flight
down the day's lengthening incline
into evening's lost dreams of rest.
In a way, this is his best moment,
when he sees all his effort,
his whole life's labour of love, of art,
dwindling into nothingness and night.

For it is the only moment of the day
when he is not pushing that intolerable thing.

"Christina Rossetti Visits North-East"

'Parting after parting
All one's life long:
It's a bitter pang, parting
While love and life are strong ...'

The brand-new mid-Victorian conservatory
of Newcastle upon Tyne's grand Central Station.
Prince of Wales plumes of steam and soot
feather like palms its curving domes of glass.

Crammed with crinolines and stove-pipe hats,
John Dobson's massive portico, Italianate,
poses blond arches in trousers of stone.
The cabs leave steaming dumps of golden dung.

The crossing-sweeper tips his cap
to a profile drifting in summer veils:
peeping from a smooth dark snood of hair
Pre-Raphaelite features of a sulky angel.

•

Parting after parting is her theme: parting
from girlhood, God and William Bell Scott
the Whitman fan, who has a way with women, but
not with her — would that he had, she prayed.

He hands her into the first-class carriage
where she leans, as if exhausted, poem-plotting,
against the dark-blue buttoned velvet.
The slammed door stuns a heart

once like a singing bird — but after
that sunny picnic on Roker Sands, something
will make her keep it caged, though singing still,
in sombre, lustrous eyes, hooded like Dante's.

A top-hatted stationmaster's consumptive whistle
trills, the train jerks out a tear.   A first line's
necklace of words collects its couplings.
The locomotive takes her by the dove-gloved hands —

    'Parting after parting
    All one's life long:
    It's a bitter pang, parting
    While love and life are strong ...'

Stations of Life

Hangars of earthbound flight,
dirigibles of glass pegged down
by cast-iron columns, gleaming rails,
quays of arrival and departure
where alone I feel at home, at ease,
a random traveller without a destination —
no ticket, no bags, no reservation —
careless of hours, of tables of time:
only in your echoing solitudes,
forever dense with others,
can I breathe and be: peculiar,
an unknown passenger, anonymous
among the nameless many,
displaced person, refugee, guest
worker out of work, defector, dissi-
decadent seeking temporary asylum
from this second-class waiting-room of life,
this vast vestibule of lost footsteps.

Central Station, Newcastle upon Tyne, 1979

Variations on a Theme by Robert Desnos

Today I went walking with a friend.
We walked by the river, under the trees,
along the beach and over the rocks
to the end of the pier with its crashing seas —
along the quaysides and the silent docks.

Today I went walking with a friend.
I showed him secret places I had always known
and told him tales that I had never told.
Our words and laughter on the wind were blown
until the night fell and the town was cold.

Today I went walking with a friend.
It was the first time we had walked together —
and the last. For I never saw his face again,
or heard his voice. And now, in lonely weather,
I walk alone, my only friend the rain, the rain.

— But once I went walking with a friend.

Homage to Wordsworth

Yours one of those voices that in my boyhood
haunted my simplicity, delivered from the cruel class
my ignorance, and set a limit to my loneliness.

Like a longed-for elder brother, you
William, took me on pilgrimages in that northern land
of moors, lakes, fells and mountains, made me see
what I had seen but never known before —
the wild crags, the torrents and the clouds,
with you, a steady and persistent wanderer
guiding my sad, impulsive ways.

The shadowed valleys and the moonlit ranges,
the pouncing rain, lake tempests and the sunny gales
of snow and hail ... all nature's elements
you showed me, and we were silent friends
finding our lost paths, sleeping in the upland farms,
waking under stars to bathe in Langdale's icy stream.

— Then too much like a father you began to speak.
The friend and brother vanished in you suddenly
and you were married, staid, domestic, dull.

Where had the lightning gone, the visionary
gleam that touched Helvellyn's peak?
Where was that voice that rang and echoed on the lake's
thundering ice, at midnight, under a mountain-loaded sky?

All, all were gone, and never again with you, romantic,
except in recollection, as you had always wanted it to be,
will the calm and violence of those discoveries come back to me.

Rydal Mount

Highwire Act

From his crow's nest perch high up
against the big top's canvas sky,
a highwire walker tests with cautious toe
the taut bathwater path of air, puts one foot
out, then the other, finding his way
as if in darkness on a glittering snail-track,
full of meanders, factitious as a maze.

Sometimes he crosses his undulating bridge
balancing a horizontal ten-foot pole, whose tips
seem to be gauging the atmospheric pressure
of the tent's spangled pools of light.
Sometimes, mid-way, the highway swerves and dips,
and he must run for his life uphill, to make
the perilous haven of the further side.

But then, with an oriental parasol
in right hand, angled at arm's length
or twirling overhead, to give him spotlight shade,
he totters out again, and with a dancing step
foxtrots to the band — an entrechat — on one
foot balances, pretends to (Ooh!) slip, but falls
only in our net of laughter and applause.

The Wandering Jew

... Faut-il partir? rester? Si tu peux rester, reste;
Pars, s'il le faut. L'un court, et l'autre se tapit
Pour tromper l'ennemi vigilant et funeste,
Le Temps! Il est, hélas! des coureurs sans répit,

Comme le Juif errant et comme les apôtres,
A qui rien ne suffit, ni wagon ni vaisseau,
Pour fuire ce rétiaire infâme; il en est d'autres
Qui savent le tuer sans quitter leur berceau ...

                                    Baudelaire

Few people have ever met me,
fewer still know my name.
Sometimes there are weeks and months
when I never speak to a soul,
and almost lose my voice.

But on those days when I go outside —
and I only go out after dark —
I pass such millions of the unknown,
and their numbers, numberless,
fill me with dread and pity.

I walk among them, disembodied,
chilled at the thought that every moment
someone who once crossed my path
has died, or is now dying somewhere —
alone and surrounded in this trance of time.

Poem to be Read with the Light off

This bright forest of a book
its foliage already spattered
with raindrop texts of blackness —
jumbled letters, dots and dashes —
leaves falling, filling with white
mists pages of whispering misprints.

The trunks of darkness thicken.
Shadows mount through flakes of soot
from undergrowths of footnotes, roots
of reference, the mines of meaning,
drifting like woodsmoke to the tops of texts,
overflowing margins, overprinting print,
swirling round the leafless boughs of lines.

The twilights deepen, and their inks
obliterate the ghosts that once were white.
— Out of a gathering dream
the signs fall like showers of dust
into the long grasses of forgetfulness,
the rustling leaves of sight
that drown their images in night.

The Midnight Carolsingers

Where are they now?
Through what centuries of dreams
they come to me, the memories
of voices singing in the dark,
singing to a waking child --
now near, now infinitely far,
like angels' voices in the back lane,
on the quayside, along the bay?

What unknown carolsingers in the snows
of midnight, in the frosts of time?
Singing of birth that is death,
of peace that is war,
of love that is hatred,
of the divine that is lost?

And where is that dark-haired midnight visitor,
come on the stroke of twelve to bring
a good new year, his trouser pockets
filled with lumps of coal, offering them
for luck, in hands black with fate?

Where are they all now?
Only these innocent memories survive.

Christmas Eve, 1991